ON AN AVERAGE DAY...

ON AN

TOM

AVERAGE DAY...

HEYMANN

FAWCETT COLUMBINE ■ NEW YORK

A Fawcett Columbine Book
Published by Ballantine Books
Copyright © 1989 by Thomas N. Heymann

Library of Congress Catalog Card Number: 89-90823
ISBN: 0-449-90453-9

Cover design by Dale Fiorillo
Text design by Mary A. Wirth

Manufactured in the United States of America
First Edition: October 1989
10 9 8 7 6 5 4 3 2 1

To my wife, Grace, who,
on an average day,
walks our dogs Allie and Grizzly,
twice.

ACKNOWLEDGMENTS

I want to thank my good friends Laurie Lathem and Lisa Daro, without whose help and insightful research I could not have completed this book. Also, to my friend and literary agent Herb Katz, who gave me the courage to begin this book, and the opportunity to finish it.

INTRODUCTION

Today's world is extremely complex. In an effort to sort out the puzzle, we have turned increasingly to statistics to help us understand and cope with the size and diversity of our environment. As a result, we are confronted by an ever-expanding array of numbers. Age, weight, crime, sports; we are assaulted by figures each and every day.

Webster's defines the word *average* as "a typical or usual level, degree, or kind." While we know that *average* does not exist in the real world, it does provide a profile of the way things are. It presents a composite of all of the atypical and unusual things that occur.

Some of the statistics in this book signal great advances. Others caution worrisome trends. Still others are just for the fun of them. In all cases, however, they provide insight into the way we live. The United States is a country of 245,898,000 persons (and increasing at the rate of 5,992 per day). Here is a glimpse of who we are . . . on an average day.

ON AN AVERAGE DAY...

ON AN AVERAGE DAY...

. . . 10,501 new Americans are born

. . . 5,937 Americans die

ON AN AVERAGE DAY...

. . . 6,567 couples are married

. . . 3,197 couples are divorced

ON AN AVERAGE DAY...

. . . 178 babies are conceived by
   artificial insemination

Of these,

. . . 96 are conceived with sperm from a
   known donor

. . . 40 are conceived with sperm from a
   sperm bank

ON AN AVERAGE DAY...

. . . 389 children are adopted

Of these,

. . . 250 are adopted by relatives

. . . 139 are adopted by strangers

. . . 25 are foreign-born

ON AN AVERAGE DAY...

. . . 1,994 babies are born to unwed mothers

. . . 2,531 babies are born by cesarean section

ON AN AVERAGE DAY...

. . . 217 sets of twins are born

. . . 5 sets of triplets are born

ON AN AVERAGE DAY...

. . . 98 babies are born away from a hospital

. . . 280 babies are delivered by midwives

ON AN AVERAGE DAY...

. . . 673,693 Americans have a birthday

ON AN AVERAGE DAY...

. . . 3 million Americans purchase
birthday presents

ON AN AVERAGE DAY...

... 8,838 Americans become teenagers

... 9,951 Americans turn 18

... 10,951 Americans turn 40

... 6,000 Americans turn 65

... 35 Americans turn 100

ON AN AVERAGE DAY...

. . . 1,648 persons emigrate to the United States

. . . 670 immigrants become naturalized American citizens

ON AN AVERAGE DAY...

... 69 persons emigrate from mainland China

... 72 emigrate from India

... 72 emigrate from the Dominican Republic

... 82 emigrate from Vietnam

... 91 emigrate from Cuba

... 98 emigrate from Korea

... 144 emigrate from the Philippines

... 182 emigrate from Mexico

ON AN AVERAGE DAY...

. . . 4,637 illegal aliens are apprehended trying to cross the U.S. border

Of these,

. . . 4,481 are Mexican

ON AN AVERAGE DAY...

. . . 548 persons successfully enter the country illegally

ON AN AVERAGE DAY...

. . . $412,104 is spent by the U.S. border
patrol ($89 per alien apprehended)

ON AN AVERAGE DAY...

. . . 39,109 pounds of marijuana are
 brought into the United States

Of this,

. . . 3,911 pounds are seized by the Drug
 Enforcement Agency

18

ON AN AVERAGE DAY...

. . . 2,239 pounds of cocaine are brought into the United States

Of this,

. . . 224 pounds are seized by the Drug Enforcement Agency

ON AN AVERAGE DAY...

. . . 23 pounds of heroin are brought into the United States

Of this,

. . . 2.3 pounds are seized by the Drug Enforcement Agency

ON AN AVERAGE DAY...

... there are 290 drug-related emergency-room incidents

Of these,

... 14 are caused by marijuana

... 15 are caused by aspirin

... 16 are caused by PCP in combination

... 23 are caused by Valium

... 37 are caused by cocaine

... 40 are caused by heroin or morphine

... 58 are caused by alcohol in combination

... 10 result in deaths

ON AN AVERAGE DAY...

... 56,061 Americans drive a car after consuming alcohol

... 133 Americans die in automobile accidents

Of these,

... 71 die in alcohol-related automobile accidents

ON AN AVERAGE DAY...

. . . 2,113 Americans die of heart disease

. . . 1,265 Americans die of cancer

. . . 419 Americans die from strokes

. . . 256 Americans die in accidents

. . . 205 Americans die from chronic
obstructive pulmonary disease

. . . 185 Americans die of pneumonia

. . . 101 Americans die of diabetes

. . . 81 Americans die in suicides

. . . 73 Americans die from chronic liver
disease and cirrhosis

ON AN AVERAGE DAY...

Of the 256 Americans who die in accidents,

... 133 die in motor-vehicle accidents

... 30 die in falls

... 15 die from drowning

... 13 die from fires and burns

... 11 die from poisoning

... 10 die from suffocation resulting from ingested objects

... 5 die in firearms accidents

... 2 die from poisoning by gases and vapors

ON AN AVERAGE DAY...

. . . 4,932 Americans are injured in work-related accidents

Of these,

. . . 82 are injured in mining accidents

. . . 438 are injured in agricultural accidents

. . . 521 are injured in construction accidents

. . . 822 are injured in manufacturing accidents

ON AN AVERAGE DAY...

. . . 30 Americans die in work-related accidents

Of these,

. . . 1 dies in a mining accident

. . . 3 die in manufacturing accidents

. . . 4 die in agricultural accidents

. . . 6 die in construction accidents

ON AN AVERAGE DAY...

. . . 3 Americans are killed accidentally by handguns

Of these,

. . . 1 is a child under the age of 15

ON AN AVERAGE DAY...

... 1 American drowns in the bathtub

... 3 Americans are killed by falling objects

ON AN AVERAGE DAY...

... 24 Americans die of AIDS

Of these,

... 4 are Hispanic

... 6 are black

ON AN AVERAGE DAY...

. . . 55 Americans die from exposure to household radon gas

ON AN AVERAGE DAY...

. . . 886 persons are cremated

. . . 4,928 persons are buried

ON AN AVERAGE DAY...

. . . 24,384 Americans suffer disabling injuries from accidents

. . . accidents cost the United States $323,287,671 in lost wages, medical expenses, insurance, fire and property damage, and indirect work loss

ON AN AVERAGE DAY...

. . . 1 American is injured by lightning

. . . 35 are injured by fireworks

. . . 68 are injured playing golf

. . . 104 are injured while shaving

. . . 153 are injured using chain saws

. . . 189 are injured using lawn mowers

. . . 307 are injured in the bathtub or shower

ON AN AVERAGE DAY...

. . . 7 Americans are injured using playpens

. . . 23 are injured using high chairs

. . . 32 are injured using strollers

. . . 38 are injured using cribs

. . . 57 are injured using walkers and jumpers

. . . 222 are injured using skateboards

. . . 1,546 are injured using bicycles

ON AN AVERAGE DAY...

. . . 523 children are treated at hospitals
for playground injuries

ON AN AVERAGE DAY...

. . . American children watch 3 1/2 hours
    of television

During which time they will see,

. . . 5 beer and wine commercials

. . . 33 acts of violence

. . . 38 sexual references and innuendos

ON AN AVERAGE DAY...

. . . 2,750 children suffer physical,
    educational, or emotional neglect

. . . 1,849 children are abused

Of these,

. . . 14 children die

ON AN AVERAGE DAY...

. . . 5,556 schoolchildren are spanked in
schools (on an average school day)

ON AN AVERAGE DAY...

. . . 4,707 children are reported missing

ON AN AVERAGE DAY...

. . . 1,932 children are abducted

Of these,

. . . 14 are abducted by strangers

ON AN AVERAGE DAY...

... 2,740 children run away from home

... 514 runaways become involved in illegal activities

Of these,

... 296 become involved in prostitution

ON AN AVERAGE DAY...

... 735,000 Americans are homeless on any given night

Of these,

... 100,000 are children under the age of 18

ON AN AVERAGE DAY...

... 2,400,000 children attend day-care centers

... 60,000 adults attend adult day-care centers

ON AN AVERAGE DAY...

. . . 133,932,656 Americans eat out

Of these,

. . . 16,300,000 eat at McDonald's

ON AN AVERAGE DAY...

. . . 1,700,000 children under the age of 6 eat at one of the hamburger chains

ON AN AVERAGE DAY...

... an average American consumes 4
    pounds of food

Of this,

... 6 ounces is red meat

... 3 ounces is poultry

... 3 ounces is corn sweetener

... 3 ounces is sugar

... 1 ounce is fish

ON AN AVERAGE DAY...

... men spend 7 minutes on childcare

... women spend 27 minutes

ON AN AVERAGE DAY...

... men spend 15 minutes preparing
   meals

... women spend 51 minutes

ON AN AVERAGE DAY...

... men spend 26 minutes cleaning
house

... women spend 59 minutes

ON AN AVERAGE DAY...

. . . men spend 20 minutes shopping

. . . women spend 38 minutes

ON AN AVERAGE DAY...

... the average family spends $13.71
   shopping for food

Of this,

... $4.86 is spent by female teenagers

ON AN AVERAGE DAY...

. . . 10,959 girls between the ages 12
and 19 go on diets

ON AN AVERAGE DAY...

. . . 101,280,321 American adults are on
   diets

Of these,

. . . 41,017,707 are men

. . . 60,262,614 are women

ON AN AVERAGE DAY...

. . . 2,739,726 Dunkin' Donuts are served

ON AN AVERAGE DAY...

. . . 17,000,000 Tootsie Rolls are
produced

ON AN AVERAGE DAY...

... 100,000,000 M&Ms are sold

Of those,

... 30,000,000 are brown

... 20,000,000 are red

... 20,000,000 are yellow

... 10,000,000 are orange

ON AN AVERAGE DAY...

... Americans eat 24,657,534 hot dogs

ON AN AVERAGE DAY...

. . . Americans drink 524,000,000
servings of Coca-Cola

ON AN AVERAGE DAY...

. . . 2,005,479 Americans suffer
heartburn

ON AN AVERAGE DAY...

... Americans spend $2,021,918 on home exercise equipment

... Americans spend $3,561,644 on tortilla chips

ON AN AVERAGE DAY...

. . . Americans spend $3,673,973 on vitamins

. . . Americans spend $10,410,959 on potato chips

ON AN AVERAGE DAY...

... Americans spend $13,698,630 on health-club membership fees

... Americans spend $21,917,808 on snack food

ON AN AVERAGE DAY...

... $1,255,342,466 is spent on health care

Of this,

... $551,095,343 goes to hospitals

... $289,984,110 goes to doctors

... $119,257,534 goes to nursing homes

... $94,150,685 goes to drugs and medical supplies

... $92,895,342 goes to dentists

ON AN AVERAGE DAY...

. . . 37,000,000 Americans don't have health-insurance coverage

. . . 2,740 lose their health-insurance coverage

. . . 2,740 are denied routine health care because they cannot pay

. . . 38,356 don't seek health care because they know they can't afford it

ON AN AVERAGE DAY...

... 99 additional American families fall
below the poverty line

ON AN AVERAGE DAY...

. . . 268 additional Hispanic families fall below the poverty line

. . . 444 additional black families fall below the poverty line

While,

. . . 619 additional white families rise above the poverty line

ON AN AVERAGE DAY...

. . . 4,110 Americans start smoking

. . . 877 Americans die of smoking-
related illnesses

ON AN AVERAGE DAY...

... $1,463,978 is spent advertising cigarettes and accessories

... 55 million Americans smoke

Of these,

... 4 million are under the age of 18

ON AN AVERAGE DAY...

... 1,562,739,726 cigarettes are sold
Of these,
... 368,767,123 are Marlboros

ON AN AVERAGE DAY...

. . . 3,288 new persons try to quit smoking using Nicorette gum

ON AN AVERAGE DAY...

. . . 4,110 Americans suffer a heart attack

. . . 1,482 Americans die from a heart attack

ON AN AVERAGE DAY...

. . . 1,109,589 condoms are sold

Of these,

. . . 443,836 are purchased by women

ON AN AVERAGE DAY...

... 3,477 abortions are performed

Of these,

... 769 are performed on women under
the age of 20

... 29 are performed on girls under the
age of 15

ON AN AVERAGE DAY...

... 48,219 Americans donate blood

ON AN AVERAGE DAY...

. . . 104 Americans learn CPR

ON AN AVERAGE DAY...

... 219,178 Americans visit the doctor because of headaches

... Americans take 80,000,000 aspirin tablets

ON AN AVERAGE DAY...

. . . Americans spend $1,369,863 on
laxatives

. . . Americans spend $1,668,493 on
hairspray

. . . Americans spend $10,958,904 on
over-the-counter pain relievers

. . . Americans spend $45,205,479 on
prescription drugs

ON AN AVERAGE DAY...

. . . 16 cases of Lyme disease are reported

. . . 35 cases of AIDS are reported

. . . 62 cases of tuberculosis are reported

. . . 502 cases of chicken pox are reported

. . . 2,468 cases of gonorrhea are reported

ON AN AVERAGE DAY...

. . . 3 Americans receive heart
transplants

. . . 4 Americans receive liver transplants

. . . 25 Americans receive kidney
transplants

. . . 96 Americans receive cornea
transplants

ON AN AVERAGE DAY...

... 8 Americans receive hair transplants

ON AN AVERAGE DAY...

. . . 1,618 Americans undergo aesthetic
plastic surgery

ON AN AVERAGE DAY...

... 183 Americans receive face-lifts

Of these,

... 18 are performed on men

ON AN AVERAGE DAY...

. . . 225 Americans receive nose jobs

Of these,

. . . 56 are performed on men

ON AN AVERAGE DAY...

... 47 women receive breast lifts

ON AN AVERAGE DAY...

... 256 women receive breast
augmentations

ON AN AVERAGE DAY...

... $46,575,342 is spent on beauty-related goods and services

... $202,739,726 is spent on low-calorie foods

ON AN AVERAGE DAY...

... Americans spend $33,561,644 buying lottery tickets

Of this,

... $16,438,356 is returned in prizes

... $12,328,767 is provided to education

ON AN AVERAGE DAY...

. . . 43,343 hunting licenses are
purchased

. . . 83,152 fishing licenses are purchased

ON AN AVERAGE DAY...

Americans purchase . . .

. . . 3,014 hockey sticks

. . . 3,562 pairs of bowling shoes

. . . 6,153 soccer balls

. . . 7,611 skateboards

. . . 8,493 basketballs

. . . 29,589 pairs of aerobic shoes

. . . 33,973 sets of golf clubs

. . . 486,575 golf balls

ON AN AVERAGE DAY...

. . . 6,619 tennis racquets are purchased

. . . 34,480 tennis racquets are restrung

Of these,

. . . 3,838 are restrung with sheep or
cow gut

ON AN AVERAGE DAY...

. . . 12 new golf holes are constructed

ON AN AVERAGE DAY...

. . . 36,910 cars are sold

Of these,

. . . 16,241 are sold to women

ON AN AVERAGE DAY...

. . . 12,630 light trucks are sold

Of these,

. . . 2,147 are sold to women

ON AN AVERAGE DAY...

. . . Christian bookstores sell 34,932
   Bibles

ON AN AVERAGE DAY...

... 890 copies of Betty and Veronica comics are sold

... 1,096 copies of Archie comics are sold

... 19,036 copies of G.I. Joe comics are sold

... 29,872 copies of Spider-Man comics are sold

... 42,155 copies of X-Men comics are sold

ON AN AVERAGE DAY...

. . . 124 new book titles are published
Of these,

. . . 9 concern medicine

. . . 12 are written for children

. . . 15 are adult fiction

. . . 18 involve sociology or economics

ON AN AVERAGE DAY...

. . . 1 new book title is published in
Braille

ON AN AVERAGE DAY...

. . . 105,108,286 Americans read a
newspaper

Of these,

. . . 27,000,000 read their horoscope

. . . 52,000,000 read the obituaries

. . . 70,000,000 read "Dear Abby"

. . . 79,250,000 read the comics

. . . 81,500,000 read the editorials

. . . 85,000,000 read Ann Landers

. . . 86,202,000 read the sports pages

ON AN AVERAGE DAY...

. . . 5,300,000 Americans read *USA Today*

ON AN AVERAGE DAY...

. . . Americans spend $272,876,712
    (buying products by mail order)

ON AN AVERAGE DAY...

... 43,081,683 credit-card purchases are made

... $1,507,858,905 worth of goods and services are charged

... 253,151 purchases are made with ATM cards

ON AN AVERAGE DAY...

. . . $3,191,353,425 is spent at retail
    stores

Of this,

. . . $1,600,000,000 is spent in shopping
    malls

ON AN AVERAGE DAY...

. . . $256,657,534 is given to charity

Of this,

. . . $12,328,767 is given by corporations

. . . $16,383,562 is given by bequests

. . . $17,479,452 is given by foundations

. . . $210,465,753 is given by individuals

ON AN AVERAGE DAY...

. . . $256,657,534 is given to charity

Of this,

. . . $17,561,644 is given to arts, culture, and humanities groups

. . . $26,958,904 is given to human-services organizations

. . . $29,698,630 is given to education

. . . $37,397,260 is given to health organizations

. . . $119,479,452 is given to religious organizations

ON AN AVERAGE DAY...

. . . 4 earthquakes measuring more than
2.5 on the Richter scale are reported

ON AN AVERAGE DAY...

... 116,438 Americans move

Of these,

... 3,260 move to Washington, D.C.

... 3,377 move to Tampa

... 3,493 move to Atlanta

... 4,658 move to New York

... 5,356 move to Los Angeles

ON AN AVERAGE DAY...

... 166 forest fires are started

Of these,

... 8 are started by burning debris

... 9 are started by smoking

... 17 are started by campfires

... 24 are started by deliberate arson

... 85 are started by lightning

ON AN AVERAGE DAY...

. . . 5,951 acres are burned by forest
fires

ON AN AVERAGE DAY...

... 811,506,849 pounds of residential and commercial trash is generated (3.5 lbs/person)

Of this,

... 59,240,000 pounds are food

... 76,281,644 pounds are glass

... 341,644,383 pounds are paper products

ON AN AVERAGE DAY...

... 81,150,685 pounds of household and commercial trash are recycled

ON AN AVERAGE DAY...

. . . 438,356,164 pounds of paper
products are consumed

Of this,

. . . 120,547,945 pounds are recycled

. . . 2,191,781 pounds are used in
nonrecyclable disposable diapers

ON AN AVERAGE DAY...

. . . 115,068,493 glass bottles and jars
    are produced

Of these,

. . . 13,698,630 are recycled

ON AN AVERAGE DAY...

. . . 657,534 automobile tires are
   produced

Of these,

. . . 197,260 are recycled

ON AN AVERAGE DAY...

. . . 93,310,137 aluminum cans are
   produced

Of these,

. . . 47,121,619 are recycled

ON AN AVERAGE DAY...

. . . 17,534,000 pounds of medical waste
    are generated

Of this,

. . . 2,191,781 pounds are infectious

ON AN AVERAGE DAY...

. . . the nation's trash consists of . . .

. . . 4,383,562 disposable pens

. . . 5,479,452 disposable razors

. . . 43,835,616 disposable diapers

ON AN AVERAGE DAY...

. . . the federal government spends
$5,479,452 under the Water Quality
Act of 1987

. . . 3 billion gallons of sewage is
dumped off the coasts of the United
States

ON AN AVERAGE DAY...

... the federal government spends
$13,424,658 on the EPA
(Environmental Protection Agency)

... air pollution causes $13,698,630 in
damage to crops

ON AN AVERAGE DAY...

. . . 2 million Americans breathe
dangerous levels of sulfur dioxide

. . . 8 million Americans breathe
dangerous levels of nitrogen dioxide

. . . 40 million Americans breathe
dangerous levels of carbon monoxide

. . . 48 million Americans breathe
dangerous levels of particulates

. . . 76 million Americans breathe
dangerous levels of ozone

ON AN AVERAGE DAY...

. . . 1,096 acres of wetlands are lost to
agriculture and development

ON AN AVERAGE DAY...

. . . there are 495 threatened and
endangered species

ON AN AVERAGE DAY...

... 30 sea turtles drown in shrimp trawl nets

... 274 dolphins are murdered by tuna fishermen

... 5,479 waterfowl die from lead poisoning

ON AN AVERAGE DAY...

... 125,455 acres of land are acquired
for addition to the national parks

ON AN AVERAGE DAY...

. . . the United States Peace Corps spends $23,014 on recruiting

. . . the United States Department of Defense spends $5,831,781

ON AN AVERAGE DAY...

... 8 Americans begin service with the Peace Corps

... 868 Americans enlist in the armed forces

ON AN AVERAGE DAY...

Of the Americans who newly enlist in the armed forces,

. . . 715 are men

. . . 99 are women

ON AN AVERAGE DAY...

... the federal government spends $459,537 on the NEA (National Endowment for the Arts)

... the federal government spends $9,863,014 on SDI (Strategic Defense Initiative)

ON AN AVERAGE DAY...

... the federal government spends
$46,027,400 on education

... the federal government spends
$807,260,270 on defense

ON AN AVERAGE DAY...

. . . members of the Armed Services and
    Defense Appropriations committees
    receive $1,370 in honorariums from
    top defense contractors

ON AN AVERAGE DAY...

... the Department of Defense awards
41,918 supplier contracts

Of these,

... 5,449 are awarded without
competitive bidding

ON AN AVERAGE DAY...

. . . the Department of Defense awards
   $428,767,123 in supplier contracts

Of this,

. . . $171,506,849 is awarded without
   competitive bidding

ON AN AVERAGE DAY...

. . . lobbying groups spend $174,301
    trying to influence Congress

Of this,

. . . the National Committee to Preserve
    Social Security spends $8,027

. . . Common Cause spends $7,014

. . . Phillip Morris spends $6,986

. . . Handgun Control Inc. spends $2,467

. . . the National Rifle Association (NRA)
    spends $1,830

ON AN AVERAGE DAY...

. . . members of Congress receive
$26,849 in speaking fees from
special-interest groups

Of this,

. . . $276 is given by Paine Webber

. . . $279 is given by the Tobacco
Institute

. . . $313 is given by the National
Association of Broadcasters

. . . $322 is given by the American
Trucking Associations

ON AN AVERAGE DAY...

... 3 government officials are indicted

... 9 arbitration cases are filed against stockbrokers

... 35 Americans are arrested on charges of embezzlement

... 957 Americans are arrested on charges of fraud

ON AN AVERAGE DAY...

. . . 2 interruptions of communication (wiretaps) are authorized

. . . 7 persons are arrested as a result of wiretap information

ON AN AVERAGE DAY...

. . . 240 cases of arson are reported

. . . 56 house fires are started by arson

ON AN AVERAGE DAY...

. . . 3,474 residential fires are reported
In these,
. . . 78 persons are injured
. . . 17 persons are killed

ON AN AVERAGE DAY...

. . . $2,191,781 is spent on home security systems

. . . 11,800 American homes are burglarized

ON AN AVERAGE DAY...

... 2,433 automobiles are stolen

... 1,704 Americans are robbed

... 3,786 Americans are assaulted

... 49 Americans are murdered

ON AN AVERAGE DAY...

. . . 126 Americans are raped

Of these,

. . . 32 are raped by two or more
   persons

ON AN AVERAGE DAY...

... 1 American is murdered by strangulation

... 3 Americans are murdered with blunt objects, clubs, or hammers

... 3 Americans are murdered with hands, fists, or feet

... 10 Americans are murdered with cutting or stabbing instruments

ON AN AVERAGE DAY...

. . . 3,562 rifles are purchased

. . . 2 Americans are murdered
with a rifle

ON AN AVERAGE DAY...

. . . 3,014 shotguns are purchased

. . . 3 Americans are murdered
with a shotgun

ON AN AVERAGE DAY...

... 3,836 handguns are purchased

... 21 Americans are murdered with a handgun

ON AN AVERAGE DAY...

... 1,719 crimes are committed against the elderly

Of these,

... 215 are assaults

... 158 are pickpocketings

... 117 are robberies

... 39 are purse snatchings

... 4 are rapes

ON AN AVERAGE DAY...

... 93,474 crimes are committed

... 34,795 Americans are arrested

... 1,593 Americans are sent to state and federal prisons

ON AN AVERAGE DAY...

. . . 3 cases of anti-Semitic violence
are reported

. . . 19 homosexuals are subjected to
harassment, threats, or violence

ON AN AVERAGE DAY...

... the Equal Employment Opportunity
Commission receives 301 complaints

Of these,

... 8 involve equal-pay disputes

... 9 involve religious discrimination

... 19 involve sexual harassment

ON AN AVERAGE DAY...

. . . 6,082 complaints are received by the
Better Business Bureau

ON AN AVERAGE DAY...

. . . 5 companies change their name

Of these,

. . . 2 do so because of a merger or acquisition

ON AN AVERAGE DAY...

. . . 9 corporate mergers occur

ON AN AVERAGE DAY...

. . . 33 new consumer products are
introduced

Of these,

. . . 6 are introduced by grocery
manufacturers

. . . 14 are introduced by toy
manufacturers

ON AN AVERAGE DAY...

. . . Americans spend $434,246,575
   on toys

ON AN AVERAGE DAY...

. . . $63,301,699 is spent on television advertising

. . . $80,547,945 is spent on newspaper advertising

ON AN AVERAGE DAY...

. . . $24,109,589 is spent on network television advertising

. . . $29,315,068 is spent on newspaper classified advertising

ON AN AVERAGE DAY...

. . . Procter & Gamble spends $1,034,521
on television advertising

. . . Phillip Morris spends $909,315

. . . McDonald's spends $592,055

ON AN AVERAGE DAY...

. . . Coca-Cola spends $546,944 on advertising

. . . 965,000 Americans drink Coke for breakfast

ON AN AVERAGE DAY...

... $3,079,814 is spent advertising beer, wine, and liquor

... $319,726,027 is lost to alcoholism and related problems in the form of lost employment and reduced productivity

ON AN AVERAGE DAY...

. . . industry loses $136,986,301 because of absenteeism and medical expenses due to headaches

. . . industry loses $547,945,206 from employee time theft

ON AN AVERAGE DAY...

. . . Americans spend 101,369,863 hours waiting in line

ON AN AVERAGE DAY...

... 958,904,110 photocopies are made
Of these,

... 356,164,384 are unnecessary

... $7,123,288 is wasted making
   unnecessary photocopies

ON AN AVERAGE DAY...

. . . 1,924 businesses are incorporated

. . . 168 businesses fail

ON AN AVERAGE DAY...

... 12 wholesale businesses fail

... 12 manufacturing businesses fail

... 18 construction businesses fail

... 33 retail businesses fail

... 66 service businesses fail

ON AN AVERAGE DAY...

... 16 new tanning salons are listed in the Yellow Pages

... 7 fewer solar-energy-equipment wholesalers are listed

... $1,232,877 is spent on sun-care products

ON AN AVERAGE DAY...

. . . 34 restaurants are opened

. . . 8 restaurants close

ON AN AVERAGE DAY...

. . . 209 bankruptcy filings are made

ON AN AVERAGE DAY...

... industry spends $1,917,808 on
   support for the arts

... industry spends $172,602,740 on
   research and development

ON AN AVERAGE DAY...

. . . not-for-profit organizations spend $4,109,589 on research and development

. . . universities spend $8,219,178

. . . industry spends $172,602,740

. . . the federal government spends $178,082,192

ON AN AVERAGE DAY...

... AT&T spends $6,849,315 on
research and development

... IBM spends $10,958,904

... General Motors spends $12,054,795

ON AN AVERAGE DAY...

... 243 patents are issued

Of these,

... 114 are issued to foreign inventors

Of these,

... 5 are issued to Canada

... 8 are issued to Great Britain

... 8 are issued to France

... 22 are issued to West Germany

... 47 are issued to Japan

ON AN AVERAGE DAY...

. . . 148 trademarks are issued

Of these,

. . . 24 are issued to foreign registrants

ON AN AVERAGE DAY...

. . . foreign ownership of U.S. assets grows by $243,342,466

. . . the U.S. government pays $445,205,480 in interest on the national debt

ON AN AVERAGE DAY...

. . . Italian ownership of U.S. assets grows by $547,945

. . . French ownership grows by $5,205,479

. . . Hong Kong ownership grows by $7,123,288

. . . Kuwaiti ownership grows by $13,150,685

. . . Canadian ownership grows by $39,178,082

. . . British ownership grows by $50,136,986

. . . Japanese ownership grows by $89,041,096

ON AN AVERAGE DAY...

. . . 214 Americans begin work at a Japanese-owned factory

ON AN AVERAGE DAY...

. . . 2,749 Americans enroll in foreign-
     language courses

Of these,

. . . 46 enroll in Chinese

. . . 64 enroll in Japanese

. . . 93 enroll in Russian

. . . 754 enroll in French

. . . 1,127 enroll in Spanish

ON AN AVERAGE DAY...

. . . 24,274 foreigners visit the United
  States

Of these,

. . . 8,466 visit from Japan

ON AN AVERAGE DAY...

. . . 13,614 passports are issued

Of these,

. . . 2,847 are issued to Americans age 60 and over

ON AN AVERAGE DAY...

. . . 3,424,658 Americans take a trip
within the United States

. . . 113,151 Americans take a trip
outside the United States

ON AN AVERAGE DAY...

... Americans travel 1,144,720,833 miles by air

... Americans travel 5,205,479,452 miles by motor vehicle

ON AN AVERAGE DAY...

. . . 38,356 commercial and private flights are made

. . . 2,515,068 taxi trips are made

ON AN AVERAGE DAY...

. . . 1,225,499 Americans fly in airplanes

. . . 3 air-traffic-controller errors are
reported

. . . 3 near-midair collisions are reported

ON AN AVERAGE DAY...

... 5,479 persons visit the Empire State
Building Observatory

... 8,493 visit the Statue of Liberty

... 20,000 visit Independence Park in
Philadelphia

... 44,384 visit Las Vegas

ON AN AVERAGE DAY...

... 643,836 visit amusement or
   recreation parks

Of these,

... 3,973 visit Dollywood

... 6,844 visit Opryland USA

... 36,986 visit Disneyland

... 71,233 visit Disney World and
   EPCOT

ON AN AVERAGE DAY...

. . . 1,658 visit the Graceland home of Elvis Presley

. . . 4 call Graceland asking to speak with Elvis

. . . 2 write to Elvis at the Graceland address

ON AN AVERAGE DAY...

... AT&T processes 75 million calls

... 123,288 calls are made to 900-
number phone-service numbers

Of these,

... 41,096 are made to dial-a-porn
numbers

ON AN AVERAGE DAY...

. . . 55 calls are made to 1-800-CALL-SPY, the army hot line established to report cases or evidence of espionage

ON AN AVERAGE DAY...

... 875 calls are made to Norman
   Vincent Peale's DIAL-A-PRAYER

ON AN AVERAGE DAY...

. . . 421,643,836 pieces of mail are sent
   via the U.S. Postal Service

Of these,

. . . 163,652,597 pieces are direct-mail
   advertising

ON AN AVERAGE DAY...

. . . 36,000,000 million stamps are
printed

ON AN AVERAGE DAY...

. . . 245,727 letters are added to the U.S. Postal Service's dead-letter file

ON AN AVERAGE DAY...

. . . 19,452,055 greeting cards are sold
Of these,
. . . 9,726,027 are sent by mail

ON AN AVERAGE DAY...

... the U.S. Postal Service delivers
113,699 overnight parcels

... Federal Express delivers 241,479

192

ON AN AVERAGE DAY...

. . . 22,500,000 currency notes are printed

Of these,

. . . 8,854,795 are $1

. . . 2,139,178 are $5

. . . 1,911,233 are $10

. . . 4,032,877 are $20

. . . 534,795 are $50

. . . 596,164 are $100

ON AN AVERAGE DAY...

. . . 34,577,534 coins are minted

Of these,

. . . 25,616,438 are pennies

. . . 1,917,808 are nickels

. . . 3,479,452 are dimes

. . . 3,561,644 are quarters

. . . 2,192 are fifty-cent pieces

ON AN AVERAGE DAY...

. . . 457,000,000 Susan B. Anthony
   dollars are being stored in U.S.
   vaults

ON AN AVERAGE DAY...

... 8,000 new members join the American Association of Retired Persons (AARP)

... 3,562 Americans are admitted to nursing homes

ON AN AVERAGE DAY...

... 623 new members join the Mormon
church

ON AN AVERAGE DAY...

... the song "Satisfaction" is played on the radio 302 times

... the song "Love Me Tender" is played 433 times

... the song "Yesterday" is played 589 times

... the song "Always on My Mind" is played 633 times

ON AN AVERAGE DAY...

. . . 139,726 cassette singles are shipped

. . . 224,658 disc singles are shipped

. . . 279,726 compact discs are shipped

. . . 293,151 record albums are shipped

. . . 1,123,288 cassettes are shipped

ON AN AVERAGE DAY...

. . . 3,360,827 items are borrowed from
public libraries

ON AN AVERAGE DAY...

. . . 1 new magazine is launched

. . . 1 new motion picture is released

ON AN AVERAGE DAY...

. . . 2,982,192 Americans attend a movie

. . . 6,301,370 videos are rented

ON AN AVERAGE DAY...

... 7,490 new homes are wired for cable television

... 1,561 new homes subscribe to the Disney Channel

... 119 homes disconnect the Playboy Channel

ON AN AVERAGE DAY...

... 51,233 cameras are sold

... 41,506,849 pictures are taken

Of these,

... 36,526,027 are taken in color

... 1,183,562 are taken on Disney
property (Disneyland, etc.)

ON AN AVERAGE DAY...

. . . 34,521 bicycles are sold

. . . 8,219 Americans take up bicycling

ON AN AVERAGE DAY...

... 498,630 cars are registered

... 4,128,767 cars are washed

ON AN AVERAGE DAY...

. . . 3,288 new dogs are registered

Of these,

. . . 288 are cocker spaniels

. . . 225 are Labrador retrievers

. . . 135 are chow chows

ON AN AVERAGE DAY...

. . . Americans spend $2,054,795 on baby food

. . . Americans spend $5,845,205 on cat food

. . . Americans spend $8,550,685 on dog food

ON AN AVERAGE DAY...

. . . 386,534 Americans visit the dentist

. . . 372,912 Americans have their teeth cleaned

. . . Americans have 538,586 cavities filled

. . . Americans have 103,414 teeth extracted

ON AN AVERAGE DAY...

... 144,658 cats visit the veterinarian

... 281,096 dogs visit the veterinarian

ON AN AVERAGE DAY...

. . . 68 animals are treated with
acupuncture

ON AN AVERAGE DAY...

. . . 11 persons report cases of ghost sightings, hauntings, or poltergeists

. . . 10 persons report cases of UFO sightings

. . . 1 person claims to have sighted Elvis Presley

ON AN AVERAGE DAY...

... 28 bowlers claim to have bowled a 300-game

... 113 golfers claim to hit holes-in-one

ON AN AVERAGE DAY...

... the president of the United States earns $547.95

... the estate of Marilyn Monroe earns $2,739.73

... the estate of Elvis Presley earns $41,095.89

... Charles Schulz earns $87,671.23

... Bill Cosby earns $95,890.41

... Michael Jackson earns $164,383.56

ON AN AVERAGE DAY...

... the Ben & Jerry Foundation donates $780 to charity

... Meals on Wheels serves 7,700 meals to homebound elderly

ON AN AVERAGE DAY...

. . . 2,160,000 Hershey's Kisses are
produced

ON AN AVERAGE DAY...

. . . 3,502 fifth-graders fall in love

SOURCES

Page 3   National Center for Health Statistics
4   Same
5   Office of Technology Assessment
6   National Committee for Adoption
7   National Center for Health Statistics
8   Same
9   Same
10   Bureau of the Census
11   *American Demographics*/Roper
12   Bureau of the Census
13   Immigration and Naturalization Service
14   Same
15   Same
16   *American Demographics*
17   Immigration and Naturalization Service
18   Drug Enforcement Agency
19   Same
20   Same
21   National Institute on Drug Abuse
22   U.S. Department of Justice
            National Center for Health Statistics
            National Council on Alcoholism
23   National Safety Council
24   National Center for Health Statistics
            National Safety Council
25   National Safety Council
26   Same
27   Federal Bureau of Investigation

28	National Safety Council
29	Centers for Disease Control
30	U.S. Public Health Service
31	Cremation Association of North America
	Casket Manufacturers Association
32	National Safety Council
33	National Oceanic and Atmospheric Administration
	Consumer Product Safety Commission
	National Safety Council
34	U.S. Consumer Product Safety Commission
35	American Association of Leisure and Recreation
36	American Academy of Pediatrics
37	Centers for Disease Control
	NBC News
38	National Center for the Study of Corporal Punishment
	USA Today
39	National Center for Missing Children
40	Same
41	Same
	Psychology Today
42	*The New York Times*
	NBC News
43	Bureau of the Census
	Time
44	*American Health*
	McDonald's
45	*The Wall Street Journal*
46	U.S. Department of Agriculture

92   Motor Vehicle Manufacturers Association
                 Market Development Associates
93   Same
94   Center for Book Research, University of
                    Scranton
95   Archie Comic Publications, Inc.
                 Marvel Entertainment
96   *Publishers Weekly*
97   Library of Congress, Braille Institute
98   MediaMark
                 The Best of Dear Abby
                 Dear Ann Landers
99   *USA Today*
100   Direct Marketing Association
101   U.S. Department of Commerce
                 USA Today
102   International Council of Shopping Centers
103   American Association of Fund-Raising Counsel
                    Trust
104   Same
105   *American Demographics*
106   Gannett/Ryder Truck Rental
107   U.S. Forest Service
108   Same
109   U.S. Department of Agriculture
110   Same
                 National Solid Wastes Management Association
111   Same
                 The Natural Baby Company

112	**National Solid Wastes Management Association**
113	**Same**
114	**Environmental Protection Agency**
115	**Same**
116	*The New York Times*
117	*Environment*
	World Water Sports Association
118	**Office of Management and Budget**
	The New York Times
119	**National Wildlife Federation**
120	**Same**
121	**Same**
122	**Environmental Defense Fund**
	Greenpeace
	National Wildlife Federation
123	**U.S. National Parks Service**
124	**U.S. Peace Corps**
	Department of Defense
125	**U.S. Peace Corps**
	Department of Defense
126	**Same**
127	**Office of Management and Budget**
128	**Same**
129	*The New York Times*
130	**Department of Defense**
131	**Same**
132	*The New York Times*
133	**Common Cause**
134	**Bureau of the Census**
135	**Same**

225

ABOUT THE AUTHOR

In addition to his work as an amateur demographer, Thomas N. Heymann is a producer of educational videos and audiocassettes. In his spare time, he also invents children's games. He holds a Bachelor of Science degree in Radio, Television, and Film from Northwestern University and a Master's in Business Administration from Columbia University. He currently resides in Chappaqua, New York, with his wife Grace, son Gabriel, and two Labrador retrievers, Allie and Grizzly.